BERKLEE
JAZZ STANDARDS
FOR SOLO GUITAR

Edited by Jonathan Feist

JOHN STEIN

Berklee Press

Editor in Chief: Jonathan Feist
Vice President of Online Learning and Continuing Education: Debbie Cavalier
Assistant Vice President of Berklee Media: Robert F. Green
Dean of Continuing Education: Carin Nuernberg
Editorial Assistants: Dominick DiMaria, Won (Sara) Hwang, Sarah Walk
Cover Designer: Kathy Kikkert

John Stein Photos by André Tanure and Kofi
Musical Transcriptions by Byron Fogo
Musical Examples Originally Notated by Andy Gabrys

ISBN 978-0-87639-136-5

DISTRIBUTED BY

HAL•LEONARD®
CORPORATION
7777 W. BLUEMOUND RD. P.O. BOX 13819
MILWAUKEE, WISCONSIN 53213

1140 Boylston Street
Boston, MA 02215-3693 USA
(617) 747-2146

Visit Berklee Press Online at
www.berkleepress.com

Visit Hal Leonard Online at
www.halleonard.com

CONTENTS

CD TRACKS

INTRODUCTION

As a lifelong musician, I have performed in many contexts, from big bands and various-sized combos to solo guitar. Solo guitar situations can range from concerts to background music in restaurants, or at functions and parties. In most of these contexts, improvisation is an important element.

Solo guitar arrangements are like airport runways, and their function is to allow the music to take off into the sky. So, the arrangements I conceive are certainly not the ultimate goal or end result, but a means to a more interesting musical end. I challenge myself always to create music that reflects a sense of wholeness—that has a beginning, a developmental section, and an ending. When I develop an arrangement, I first harmonize the tune's melody and then improvise additional choruses using melodic phrases, chords or parts of chords, bass lines, and so forth. Usually, the harmonic structure of the tune provides me with the improvisational basis, although it is very interesting to use melodic content or rhythmic motifs as well. As a solo guitarist, I try to play multiple roles simultaneously, or at least give the impression of multiple roles. I try to be both the lead voice and my own accompanist.

Jazz requires a strong knowledge of theory. There have been a number of uniquely special musicians who play solely by ear. But most of us don't have the kind of talent to depend only on the ear, and it is very helpful to learn as much music theory as possible. All great jazz musicians use musical theory when they play, whether they understand it intellectually or simply with their intuition and their musical ears. In order to learn theory sufficiently to play jazz, it has to be absorbed to such an extent that it becomes part of who we are. We must be able to simply use it when we need it without having to think about it. To make music theory second nature, a student needs to work on foundational materials—key signatures, scales, and chord formulas, which constitute the building blocks for musical constructions—until they become automatic. If the foundation is strong, a musician can build a sophisticated and impressive musical structure and do so spontaneously during improvisation. The students I see who become successful musicians are the ones who take the time to master the foundational materials. They find it easy to add more knowledge because they have something substantial to build upon.

So, theory is important, but this book is not a systematic theory text! It is more than a batch of solo guitar arrangements, however. I have tried to share some of the musical thinking that went into the creation of the arrangements. The more theory knowledge one has, the more the supportive materials will prove valuable. My hope is that the arrangements in this book prove fun to learn and to perform, and that they provide some of the necessary tools to help you create musical arrangements of your own.

Music is a lifelong pursuit. The studying and practicing never really end, as long as you remain interested. I spend as much time practicing as I possibly can. The fact is, I love thinking about music, and I love the challenge of trying to improve myself. I learn tunes. I learn solos that other great musicians have played. I analyze the compositions of other musicians. I study types of music, and the great players and composers in each style. I study the great instrumentalists on all the different instruments, not just the guitar. I read biographies and autobiographies of great musicians. I read about the historical periods of jazz music. I hang out with musicians as much as possible and try to learn whatever they can teach me. Of course, I also work specifically on guitar technique: scales, chord voicings, and so forth. My teaching life is also a great source of valuable practice time, because I am constantly reinforcing basic concepts and foundational elements that allow me to express myself when I play.

I wish to express my gratitude and appreciation to Ed Benson, who published these arrangements in his magazine, *Just Jazz Guitar*; to Byron Fogo who transcribed and expertly notated the arrangements; to Andy Gabrys who helped me create many of the supporting materials; and to Jonathan Feist of Berklee Press, who helped me prepare the book for publication.

It is my sincere hope that these guitar arrangements will prove interesting and useful.

All the best!

John Stein

www.johnstein.com

Dedicated to You

"Dedicated to You" has been recorded by many vocalists and jazz musicians, among them Nat "King" Cole, Sarah Vaughan, Ella Fitzgerald, Sammy Davis Jr., Al Hibbler, Billy Eckstine, Freddie Hubbard, and Keith Jarrett. My favorite rendition is the collaboration of John Coltrane with the singer Johnny Hartman. Their 1963 recording has marvelous performances of six great standard tunes, "Dedicated to You" among them, and it is generally considered an essential addition to a jazz record collection.

UNDERLYING HARMONY

"Dedicated to You" is written in typical AABA form. Since the A sections are heard multiple times, I wanted to play something a little different each time. Let's look first at the harmony in the A sections, which forms the basis for the variations:

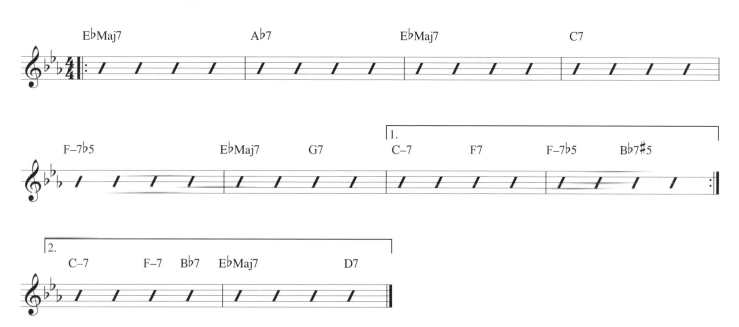

ANALYSIS OF THE ARRANGEMENT

During the first A section, the arrangement stays pretty close to the basic harmony, adding only a few extra chords. In measure 3, for example, the D7(♯9) chord on beat 2 creates musical tension that leads to the G–7 chord on beats 3 and 4, which in turn nicely sets up the C7 chord in measure 4. The G♭7 is added on beats 3 and 4 of measure 4 as an extra cadential chord. Both C7 and G♭7 lead to the F–7♭5 chord in measure 5. These dominant 7 chords are referred to as "substitute dominants," or as "tritone substitutions." Essentially, dominant chords built upon roots that are a tritone apart create an expectation of resolution to the same chord. C7 resolves down a fifth to the F–7♭5 chord, and G♭7 resolves down a half step to the same F–7♭5 chord.

The second A section (beginning on measure 9) is a reharmonization organized around a descending bass line. The first chord in measure 9, C–7, is a tonic substitute for the E♭ chord (C–7 is another way to think of an E♭6 chord), and then the line descends chromatically all the way to the F–7♭5 chord in measure 13. The descending bass line is harmonized with chords that keep the music moving by creating and resolving tension (B♭7 to the A–7, A♭7 to the G–7, and so forth).

In the final A section, (beginning on measure 25), instead of adding or substituting harmony, the melody is played in double-stops with the second note a sixth below. In measure 27, the melody is played in double-stops again, this time starting with a unison G followed by a unison F, each note played simultaneously on two strings with a bit of a finger stretch. The final A section utilizes a simpler harmonic approach. Sometimes, it is really effective to follow a "less is more" concept, after continually looking for ways to add more harmony in the other sections of the arrangement.

The B section of the tune, which begins at measure 17, features modulations to two different keys: first, the key of G major, followed by a modulation to the key of B♭ major, before the tune returns to the original key of E♭ for the final A section. The B section stays close to the basic harmony, but uses voicings that contain interesting "color" notes, in addition to the chord tones. These extra notes, referred to as "tensions" (or "extensions"), are available to be used in voicings and are also excellent choices for melody notes when composing or improvising. In order to know which notes can be used for this purpose, a musician can study chord scales. Each chord scale contains the actual chord tones, which on most chords are stacked in intervals of a third, as well as additional notes that fill the spaces in between the chord tones. The notes in between will be either available tensions, if they are consonant with the chord tones and reinforce the chord's function, or harmonic avoid notes, if they clash with the chord tones or otherwise obscure the chord's meaning in a progression. A thorough study of chord scales gives a composer, arranger, and improviser incredible tools for making musical decisions.

The Ending

I must admit that the ending of this arrangement is a bit of a private joke, but I'll let you in on it! Years ago, while recording one of my early CDs (*Portraits and Landscapes*), I included a performance of one of my favorite jazz standards, "Moonlight in Vermont," which has an ending everyone plays when they perform the tune. In fact, there are even lyrics written for the ending, so I'm sure that the song's composers, Karl Suessdorf and John Blackburn, wrote the ending phrase right into the tune. The lyrics for the ending phrase are: "You and me and moonlight in Vermont." Anyway, we were in the recording studio, and when we got to the ending, I substituted the final A section of "Dedicated to You" for the normal "Moonlight in Vermont" ending. Since I owe the music-loving world an ending to "Moonlight in Vermont," I thought I'd better use it on my arrangement of "Dedicated to You." It just seems to have the proper symmetry. So if you learn to play this arrangement, you can sing "You and me and moonlight in Vermont" when you get to measure 32!

Track 1

Dedicated to You

Arranged by
John Stein

Words and Music by Sammy Cahn,
Saul Chaplin and Hy Zaret

Very freely

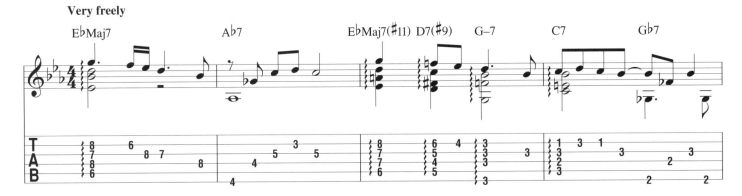

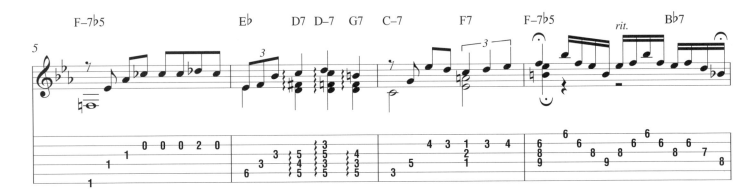

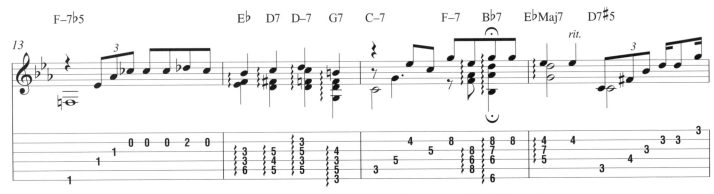

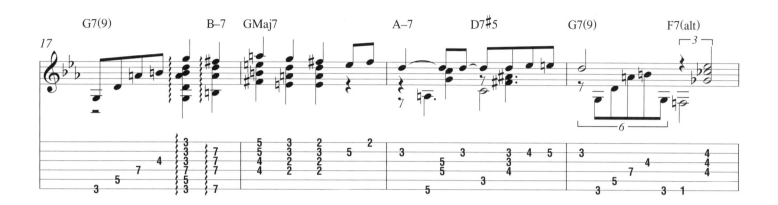

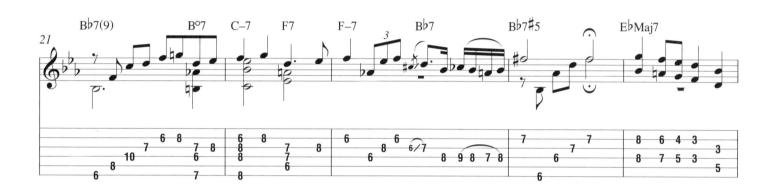

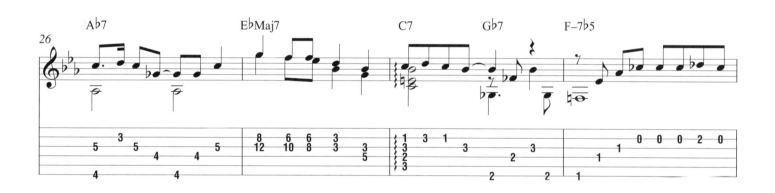

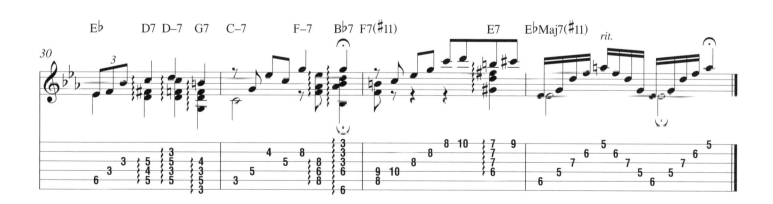

CHAPTER 2

Duke Ellington's Sound of Love

Charles Mingus is certainly one of the towering historical figures in jazz music. He was a pioneer on the string bass, a visionary composer, bandleader, and larger-than-life personality. He was artistically uncompromising, opinionated, and outspoken. His bands emphasized collective improvisation, and he chose musicians as much for their personalities and interactive qualities as for their musical skills. His compositions avoid categorization, combining elements of swing, bop, hard bop, gospel, free jazz, and classical music.

I think it is safe to say that many jazz guitarists have not delved deeply into Mingus's music. Comfortable with the elegant melody and harmony of Cole Porter, Richard Rogers, Harold Arlen, and the like, guitarists have perhaps been intimidated by the ambitious and genre-spanning nature of Mingus's personality. Can jazz guitarists play the music of Charles Mingus? Is it too difficult to reproduce on a guitar? I think it is a great potential source for musical exploration, and guitarists should give it a try.

For all of its sophistication, "Duke Ellington's Sound of Love" is melodic, highly memorable, and accessible. It is a sophisticated melody, because most of the notes are not chord tones, but rather the extensions of the chords. Yet, my first and strongest reaction to the tune is that the melody is easy to hear and easy to remember. The form of the tune is "through-composed." In other words, although the phrases fall into clear sections, the tune doesn't use a typical repetitive template, like AABA or ABAC. A few ideas are repeated, like the chromatically descending chords that harmonize the ascending melody in measures 12–13 and measures 30–31. It is interesting for me to think Mingus may have been quoting from Duke Ellington's great musical partner Billy Strayhorn in these measures. The same melodic phrase and its harmonization are found at the end of Billy Strayhorn's famous tune "Lush Life." Mingus also wrote wonderful lyrics for this composition that express his great admiration for Duke Ellington.

Track 2

Duke Ellington's Sound of Love

Arranged by
John Stein

By Charles Mingus

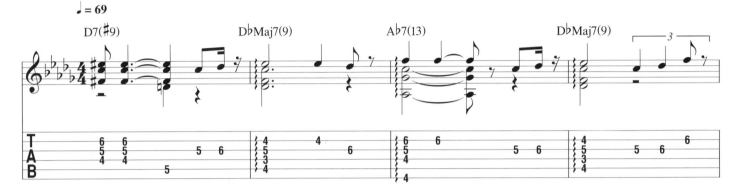

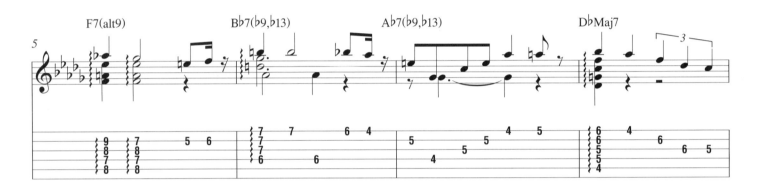

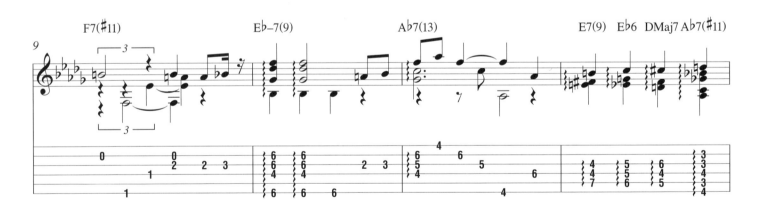

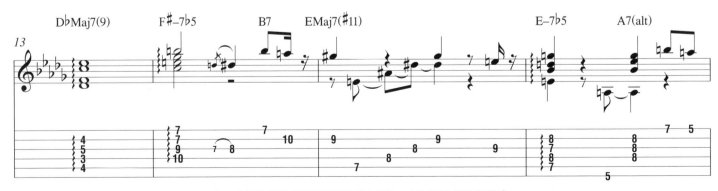

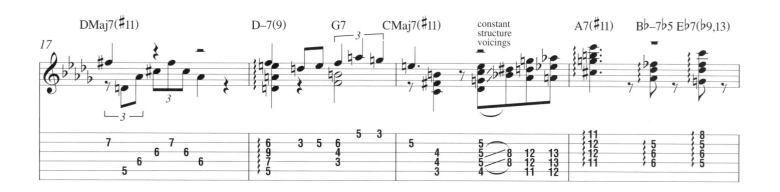

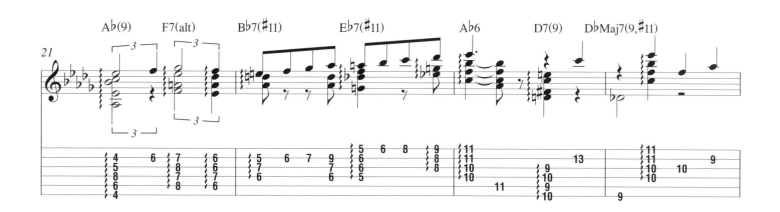

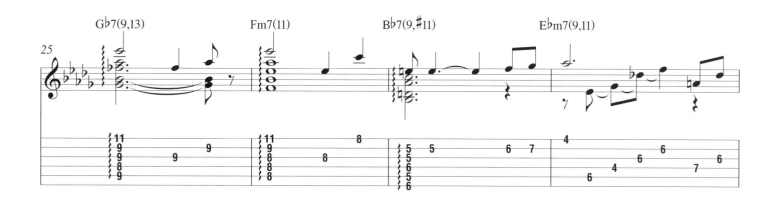

CHAPTER 3

I'm Glad There Is You

This is a one-chorus arrangement of a special tune. "I'm Glad There Is You" is one of those rare songs in which the lyrics complement the music perfectly and add immeasurably to the tune's value. The musical elements are certainly of the greatest interest to me when I create an arrangement, but when the lyrics are heartfelt and meaningful, they deepen my understanding of the tune, and I try to express them through the music. Here are the lyrics for "I'm Glad There Is You."

In this world of ordinary people, extraordinary people, I'm glad there is you.
In this world of overrated pleasures, of underrated treasures,
I'm so glad there is you.
I live to love, I love to live with you beside me.
This role so new, I'll muddle through with you to guide me.
In this world where many, many play at love, and hardly any stay in love,
I'm glad there is you.
More than ever, I'm glad there is you.

As I discussed in the introduction to this book, I like a musical arrangement to have a continuous sense of forward motion, with a beginning, middle, and end. Most arrangements have some kind of introduction. This time, I wanted to create the impression of an intro without actually playing one. The arrangement begins right on the melody of the tune and plays the first phrase (four bars), as it says on the music, "Slowly and very freely." The tempo begins in measure 5 with a medium-bright, straight-eighths feel. At the end, the arrangement returns to the freer and slower tempo, and extends the tune by two bars utilizing a deceptive cadence (B–7♭5 in measure 31 instead of the expected FMaj7), and then descends to the final tonic chord by chromatic root motion.

I'm Glad There Is You
(In This World of Ordinary People)

Arranged by
John Stein

Words and Music by Paul Madeira
and Jimmy Dorsey

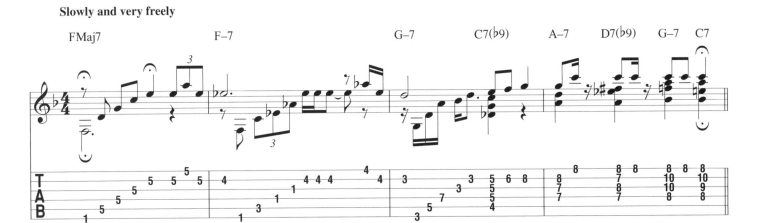

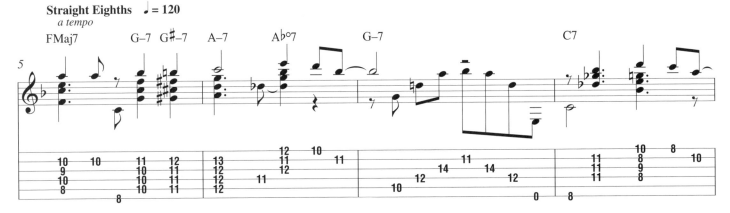

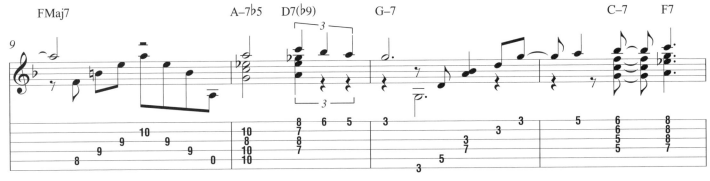

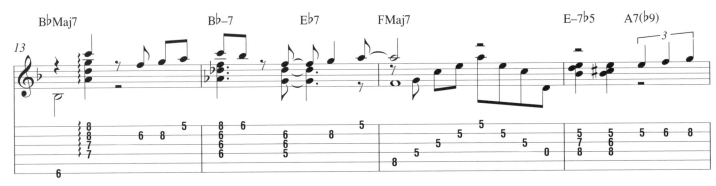

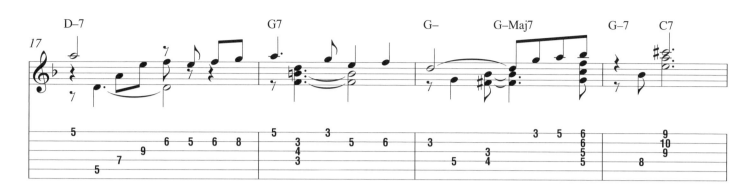

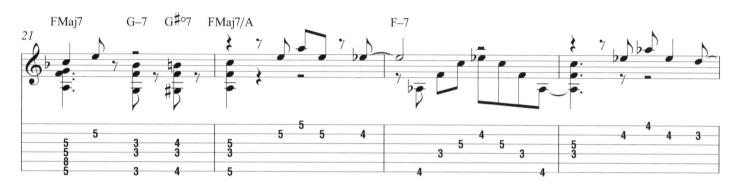

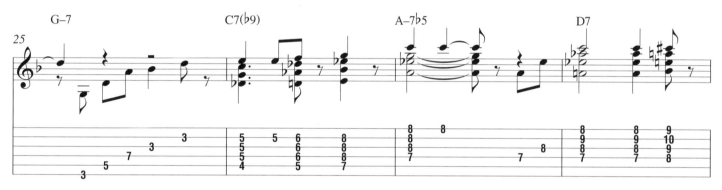

Slower and more freely

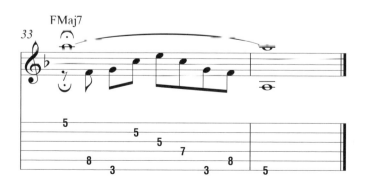

In a Sentimental Mood

COMMON CHARACTERISTICS OF MINOR KEY TUNES

The sound of minor chords is dark and emotional, so tunes written in a minor tonality have a built-in "advantage" over music in major keys. The sound of the minor triad is compelling and instantly creates a mood. Because the tonic chord in a minor key has this powerful emotional effect, minor key tunes need less sophisticated harmony to be effective. As a consequence, minor key tunes tend to have simpler chord progressions than those written in major keys, and cadences in minor key tunes tend to be basic. Another characteristic of many minor key tunes is a brief modulation in some section of the tune to a major key for contrast. As we shall see, "In a Sentimental Mood" exhibits both of these characteristics very clearly.

The musical term "cadence" refers to creating and resolving tension, and all music is filled with cadences of various types. The tonic chord in a tune is the chord that sounds the most stable compared to others, and as a consequence defines the tonal center. When music modulates and the tonic chord changes, all other harmony in the tune is reorganized.

SONG FORM

When learning a new tune, it's important to determine the song form. "In a Sentimental Mood" is written in perhaps the most common song form for jazz standards: 32 bar AABA. There is obviously a lot of repetition in an AABA tune (three of the sections are the same, or nearly so). Composers have a number of musical tools to insure that a tune with so much repetition does not become predictable or boring, but they nearly always write their B sections with contrast in mind. Duke Ellington's solution in "In a Sentimental Mood" is to modulate to a major key which is far away from the tonality of the A sections. So, the A sections of "In a Sentimental Mood" are in D minor/F major, and the B section is in the key of D♭ major.

HARMONIC ANALYSIS

If we analyze the underlying harmony in the A section of "In a Sentimental Mood," we see D minor, the I minor chord, in measures 1 and 2; G minor, the IV minor chord, in measures 3 and 4; a return to D minor in measure 5. In measure 6, we see D7 and A♭7. These chords are secondary dominants, which are nondiatonic dominant 7th chords that create tension that we expect to resolve to a diatonic chord—in this case, the G minor chord.

In a Sentimental Mood
Harmonic Analysis: A Section

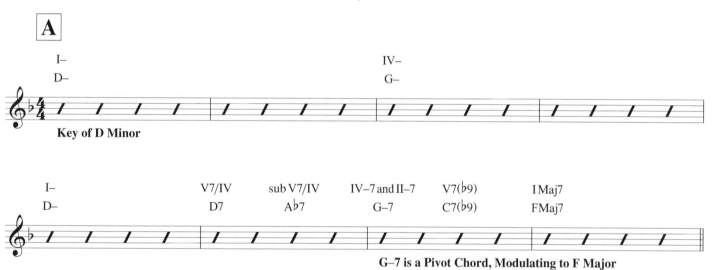

The last two bars of the A section require some attention. The secondary dominants in the preceding measure create an expectation of G minor, which we have already experienced as a IV minor chord. This time, however, the G–7 chord functions as a pivot chord—a chord with a relationship to both the original key and to a new key when the progression is modulating, and which eases the transition to the new key. It is the IV minor chord in D minor, as well as the II minor chord in the new key of F major. Duke Ellington has given us something extra in this tune: a quick modulation to F major (relative major of D minor) to end each A section.

The B section of the tune (measure 24 of the arrangement) is in the key of D♭ major. The progression is very basic: variations of I VI II V. When the tune modulates to D♭ major, the melody at that point is written with accidentals but the key signature remains the same, which is typically how a brief modulation within a tune is notated. The last two measures of the B section in this arrangement are a direct modulation to the key of A minor/C major. "In a Sentimental Mood" normally returns to the original key for the final A section, so the additional modulation was my choice as an arranger.

In a Sentimental Mood
Harmonic Analysis: B Section

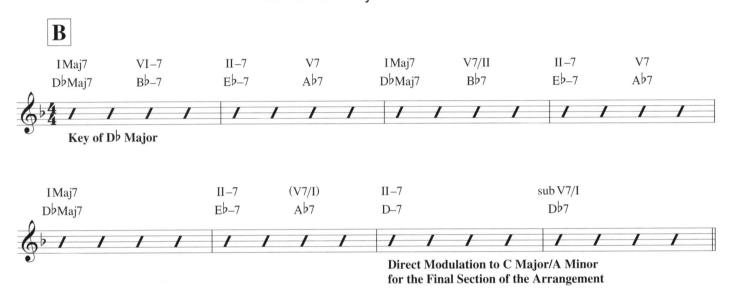

Line Cliché

Since the progression is very basic in the A sections of the tune, Duke Ellington turned to a clever device that works really well with simple harmony: the line cliché. A line cliché is a melodic phrase that gives an impression of harmonic change when there isn't any. The D minor is a tonic chord and lasts two measures. The notes D, C♯, C, B are part of a melodic phrase that descends throughout the duration of the D minor chord. The melodic phrase gives a sense of motion and change, yet does not alter the harmonic meaning of the chord. Duke uses the same device on the G minor chord in the third and fourth measures of each A section, transposed for the chord, using the melody notes G, F♯, F.

Since "In a Sentimental Mood" is an AABA tune, the line clichés occur often: on the I minor and the IV minor chords in the first four measures of every A section. One of my challenges as an arranger was to find fresh ways to play the same idea. You will see that each occasion of the line cliché is played in a different manner, changing octaves and embellishments. For even more contrast, the final A section (measure 31) is transposed to another key: A minor. In this arrangement, "In a Sentimental Mood" ends in A minor/C major.

Intro and Ending

For an intro, I borrowed a melodic phrase from the B section of the tune and transposed it to another key (DMaj7), varied it slightly, and transposed it again (to GMaj7), and repeated this process once more through the cycle of fifths (CMaj7 and FMaj7), ending with the cadence G–7 C7♯5 in the key of F major. As we have seen, Duke Ellington ends each A section in the key of F major, so ending the introduction in that key sets up the tonality for the beginning of the tune.

Another word about the introduction: it is 7 measures long! Most musicians who work with these kinds of tunes use a regular number of measures for an intro: 2, 4, or 8 bars, typically. When Byron Fogo transcribed my performance of this arrangement, I noticed to my surprise that the intro is only 7 measures long. I studied it to see if it could be written differently. Indeed, Byron notated the intro in the best possible way. The intro is only 7 measures, yet it feels "right," so it serves to remind that less common solutions to musical problems are sometimes very good choices.

The ending of the arrangement begins at measure 38. Measures 38 and 39 use voicings derived from the symmetrical dominant chord scale (half step/ whole step).

| I | T♭9 | T♯9 | 3 | T♯11 | 5 | T13 | ♭7 | 8 |

This scale, like its mirror image (whole step/half step, which is used on diminished 7 chords), has a unique and special sound. It is not closely related to any tonal center, so what one hears are the repeating patterns of exact intervals. If you want to sound close to the tonality of the tune, it would be a poor choice, but if you are interested in the special effect that the repeating exact intervals provide, it can be effective. I wanted the ending to stand out clearly from the body of the arrangement, so voicings derived from this scale were an appropriate choice. Symmetrical dominant voicings are very easy on the guitar, by the way. You simply grab one of the convenient voicings and ascend a half step (one fret) followed by a whole step (two frets) without changing your fingering. For diminished 7 chords, the same voicings work, but you would start with a whole step followed by a half step.

Track 4

In a Sentimental Mood

Arranged by
John Stein

By Duke Ellington

Very freely

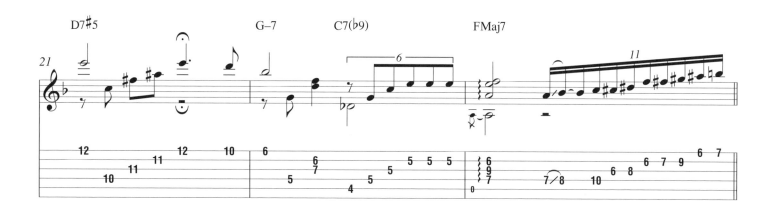

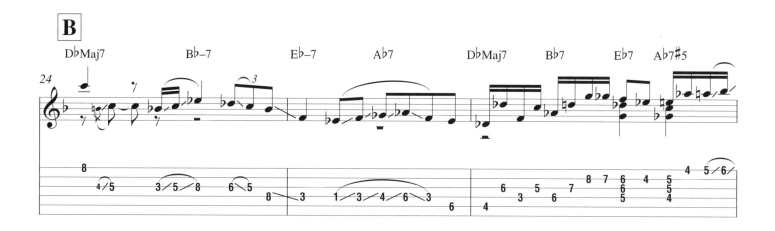

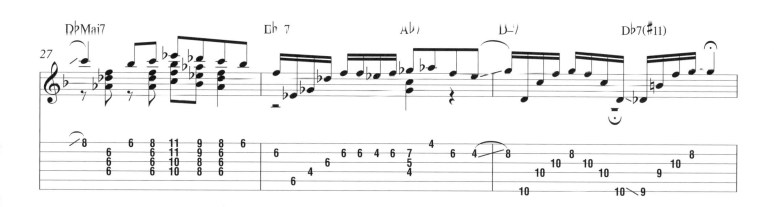

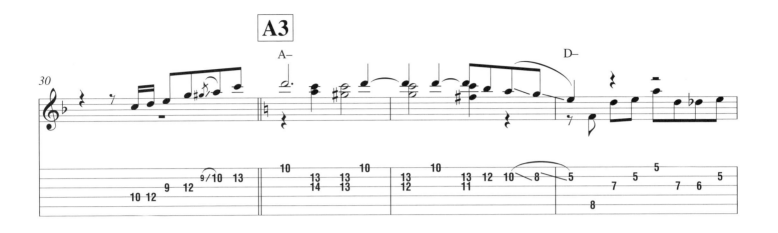

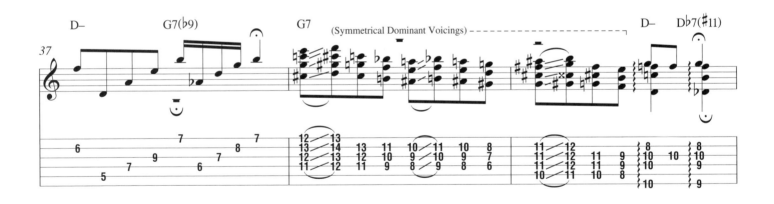

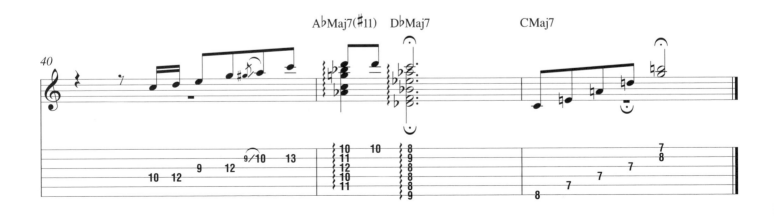

CHAPTER 5

Little Girl Blue

The first thing to mention about this wonderful tune is its unusual form. The first twelve bars are a verse, not really part of the tune. Yet nearly everyone who plays or sings this song performs the verse. It seems an intrinsic and important part of the tune, in a way that many verses are not, so it seemed important to include it in the arrangement. The arrangement returns to the beginning of the verse to form the first part of the ending.

The chorus of the tune is highly unusual. The form is a version of the AABA song form. The initial A sections are 12 measures in length, with an 8-measure B section and a final A section that is only 4 bars long. Very distinctive!

Notice the chord voicings in the sixth measure of both the intro and the ending. There aren't standard chord symbols in those measures, and instead the chords are referred to as "constant structure voicings."

Let me explain what happens when I create a solo guitar arrangement of a tune like this, and then I'll let you know how I chose to use constant structure voicings.

When I learn a tune, I look at the melody and the basic harmony that is on a lead sheet and play through the tune, searching for ways to embellish the melody or harmony in a personal way. I am very partial to richer-sounding voicings filled with the colorful nonchord tones. After a while, as I begin to evolve my preferred approach to a tune, I cease looking at the lead sheet with its "standard" chords and begin internalizing a personal version of the melody and harmony.

After I perform, record, and transcribe the music, I add chord symbols to the arrangement for the final version that will be published. I have made a philosophical decision not to worry too much about specifying all of the color notes in the chords, so usually, I use just the basic chord symbols even though most of the chords contain extension 9, 11, and/or 13. Usually, the basic chord symbols work just fine to explain the essential harmony in the arrangement. Once in a while, the chords I choose are not derived from the harmony on the original lead sheet. This is the situation in the sixth measure of the intro and the ending. Try as I might later, I could not find a way to use standard chord symbols to describe my voicings because the notes in the chords just don't fit the standard chord symbols.

I happen to love the symmetrical dominant chord scale, otherwise known as the half-step/whole-step scale. The ending of the previous arrangement, "In a Sentimental Mood," features voicings derived from this scale on a G7 chord. In this arrangement, the voicings in the sixth measure are primarily derived from a D7 symmetrical scale.

| 1 | T♭9 | T♯9 | 3 | T♯11 | 5 | T13 | ♭7 | 8 |

I harmonized the melody with abstract sounding chords, all with the same fingerings and constant structure, and I didn't concern myself about whether the chords were "correct." It interests me that I did not discover what I was doing until I tried to name the chords in the transcription, after the fact. At that point, I realized that I had harmonized the melody by ear, with musical ideas that appealed to my personal taste, rather than being guided by what the lead sheet suggested.

Track 5

Little Girl Blue

Arranged by
John Stein

Words by Lorenz Hart
Music by Richard Rodgers

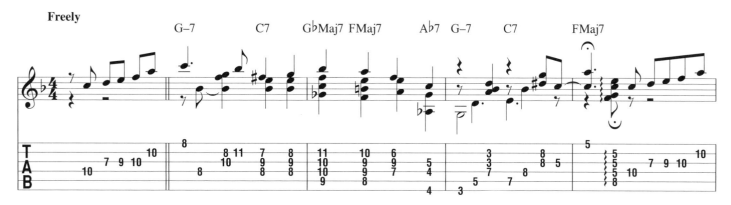

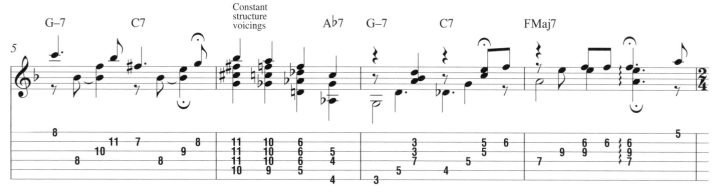

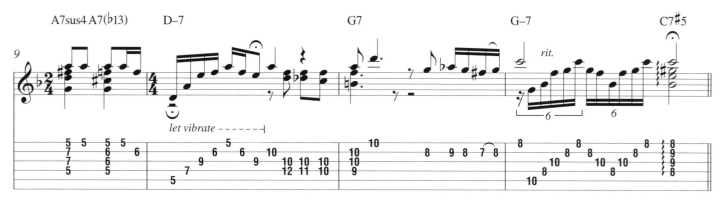

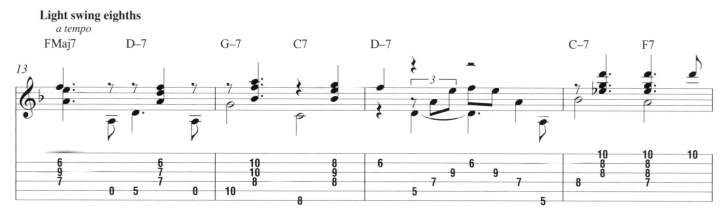

My Foolish Heart

There are a few songs, among the many I have learned and loved in my life as a musician, that simply have more emotional impact upon me. These are songs that touch me deeply whenever I play them or hear others play them. It may be that they are composed with more grace than most, or it may be that some seminal performance of the song has instantly and forever transformed it for me. One of these songs is "My Foolish Heart," by Ned Washington and Victor Young, and I suspect that both of these elements contribute to my response to the tune.

"My Foolish Heart" is well written, of course. The song form is ABAC. The melody in the A section of the tune is based upon ascending arpeggios of the diatonic chords—a simple but powerful idea. The B section descends from the highest melodic point stepwise right down the scale, to set up the repetition in the second A section. The C section somehow manages to resolve the melodic tension of the earlier melodic material. The small C–7 arpeggio at the end of the tune (measure 29), with its echo of the earlier melodic material, ties everything together.

The harmony is rich and also a bit open-ended. I have played the tune with many musicians, and everyone seems to have his or her own variation of the chords. It is interesting to me that all the versions of the harmony I have heard sound good. I guess you can dress "My Foolish Heart" up in any harmonic clothes you want, and she'll still be a graceful lady.

I have two favorite performances of "My Foolish Heart." One is Bill Evans' from his recording *Waltz for Debby*. It was recorded live at the Village Vanguard in 1961 with probably his most famous trio, including Scott LaFaro on bass and Paul Motian on drums. This rendition features an elastic time feel and a slow but swinging tempo, and its power lies in its utter conviction. Not many musicians have the ability to leave so much space at a slow tempo, and simply breathe together. Bill's early trio is renowned for its telepathic communication, and when you listen to this performance, it is easy to understand how special a group this was.

My absolute favorite version of "My Foolish Heart" is by Lenny Breau, circa 1986. It was released on a recording called *The Living Room Tapes*, and although the recording is primarily a duet consisting of Lenny and the clarinetist Brad Terry, Lenny plays a solo version of this tune. He not only plays it beautifully, but sings it as well, and his performance is totally arresting. His singing reminds me of Louis Armstrong (although their vocal quality is nothing alike), in the sense that both forget the lyrics occasionally and simply compensate by scatting something until the lyrics return. Both have nonsingers' voices, and yet use their nontraditional singing voices with such musical grace and natural phrasing that they totally sell their versions of a tune. Lenny's guitar playing is virtually on another plane. He had an ability to both play a tune and accompany himself simultaneously that I have never heard another guitarist equal. Lenny had an incredible pastel harmonic palate and the most amazing sense of time. What a guitarist!

My arrangement of "My Foolish Heart" is a tribute both to the composers and to the two musicians I mentioned, Bill Evans and Lenny Breau.

My Foolish Heart

Arranged by
John Stein

Words by Ned Washington
Music by Victor Young

Very freely

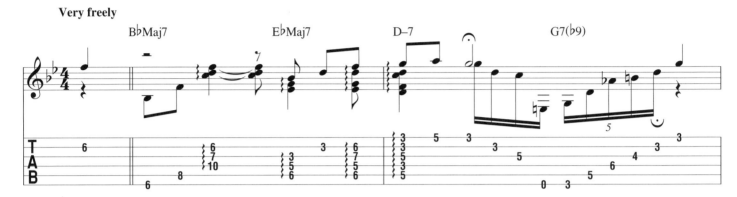

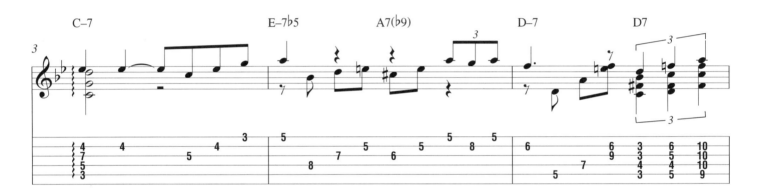

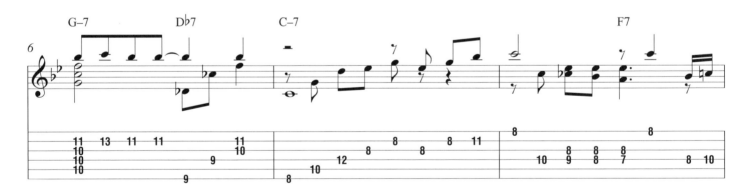

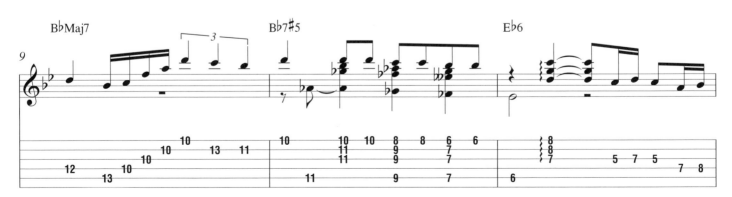

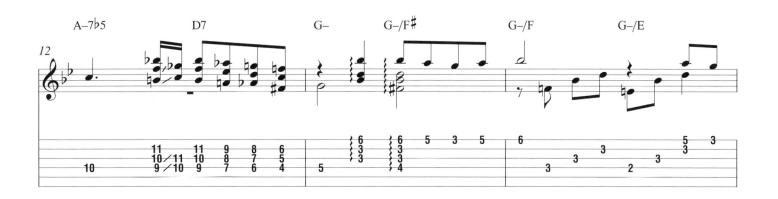

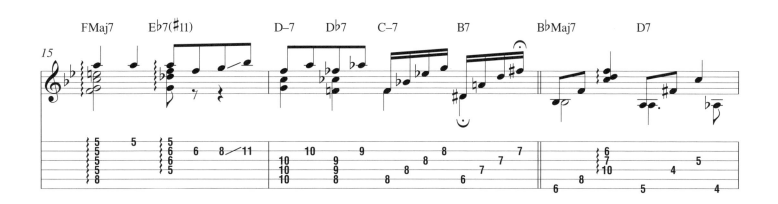

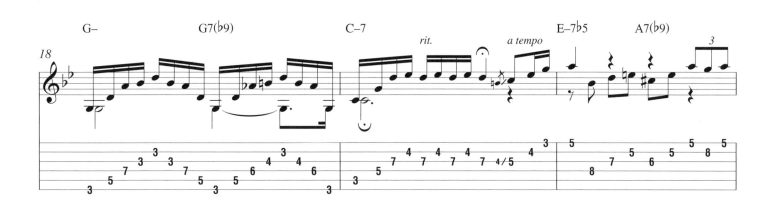

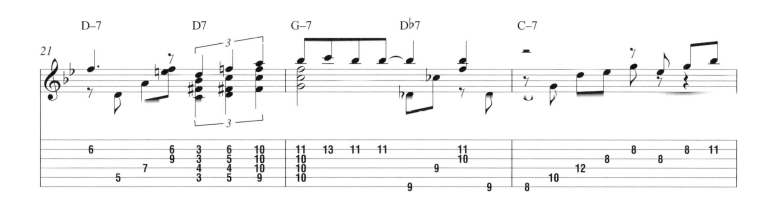

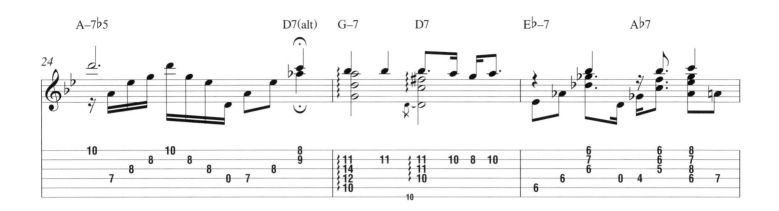

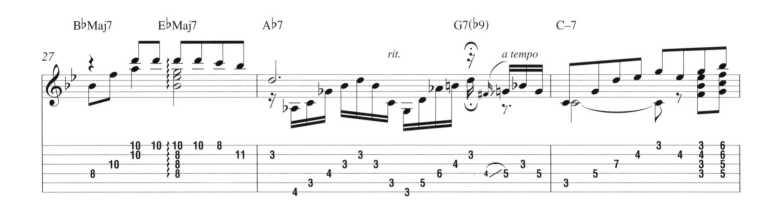

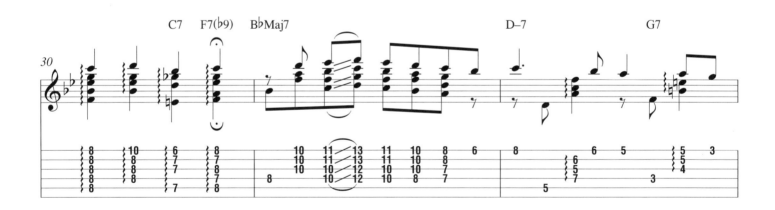

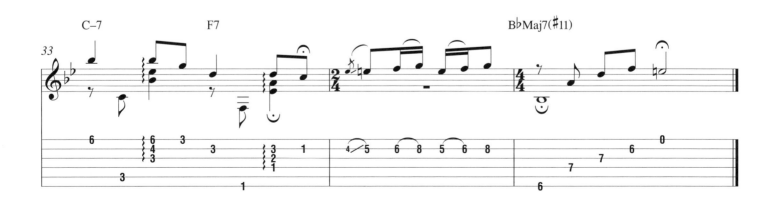

My Romance

"My Romance" is one of many Rodgers and Hart masterpieces. It is rich harmonically and melodically, and the lyrics are excellent. As a guitarist, I normally choose tunes based upon their musical content. It's a bonus if the lyrics are meaningful, and the lyrics to "My Romance" have always resonated with me. Maybe it's the line about soft guitars?

No month of May, no twinkling stars, no hide away, no soft guitars...

If a love affair is wonderful enough to dispense with the soft guitars, it must truly be "A Fine Romance" (apologies to Jerome Kern).

This performance of "My Romance" begins with a simple device: playing the melody in two different octaves. The pickup to the first measure is played on the fifth string in the lower octave, and then the melody continues an octave higher. It is easier to harmonize melodies on the top strings, placing chord tones and color notes underneath, but I try not to neglect the lower octave on the guitar.

In measures 5 and 6, the arrangement adds extra harmony. As a comparison, here are the basic chord changes in those measures:

This kind of harmonic movement is a line cliché. The G minor chord lasts for two measures, and in order to give the impression of more harmonic activity, a chromatic descending line is played. The notes in the line—G, F♯, F natural on the G–7 chord, and E on the G–6 chord—do not change the harmonic meaning of the G– chord or affect its usage in the progression. They simply make the music more interesting, because there is movement in one of the voices.

Let's take this a step further by adding more harmony. I compressed the line cliché into a single measure (measure 5) and stole an idea from the original harmony of the tune for the next measure. The first chord in measure 6 has the root E♭, which is a continuation of the descending G– line cliché (G, F♯, F natural, E), but beyond that, the chords echo the harmony in measures 1 and 2: C–7, D–7, D♭°7. In both measures 1 and 2, where we first hear the progression, and in measure 6 where it echoes, the chords lead to a C–7 F7 cadence to the B♭Maj7 chord.

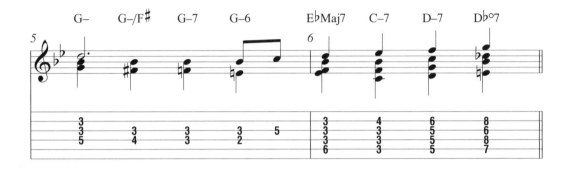

The form of "My Romance" is ABAC. It's good to treat a situation that recurs differently the second time. Let's look at the same two measures the next time they appear in the tune:

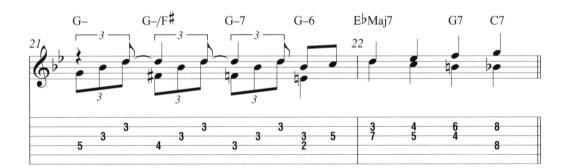

In measure 21, the G minor line cliché appears again, but this time arpeggiated for contrast. Measure 22 is also based upon a descending line (D, C, B natural, B♭), plus a simultaneous ascending line (D, E♭, F, G) moving in contrary motion. The ascending line is the actual melody to the tune. Lines moving in opposite directions are powerful musical tools, and they sound wonderful.

Let's look at one more place in "My Romance" where the arrangement uses lines to guide the performance: measures 17 and 18.

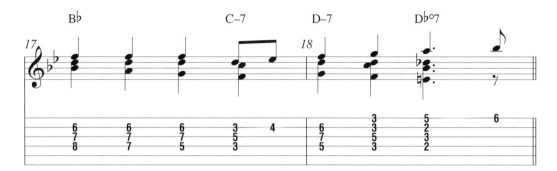

These are the first two measures of the second A section, and the chords there feature descending notes in the bottom voice (Bb, A, G, F in measure 17 and G, F, E in measure 18). In measure 18, the descending bottom voice also moves in contrary motion to the melody in the top voice.

Melodic lines that ascend and descend through chord progressions are often referred to as *guide tone lines*. It's good to use these as arranging devices in tunes like "My Romance," and they are also useful as targets of melodic phrases in improvisation. Guide tone lines help create melodies that are consonant and integrated with the chord progressions of tunes.

Track 7

My Romance

Arranged by
John Stein

Words by Lorenz Hart
Music by Richard Rodgers

Freely

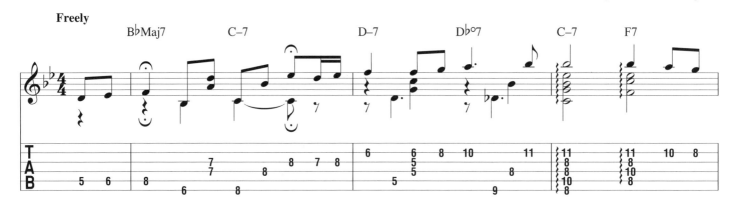

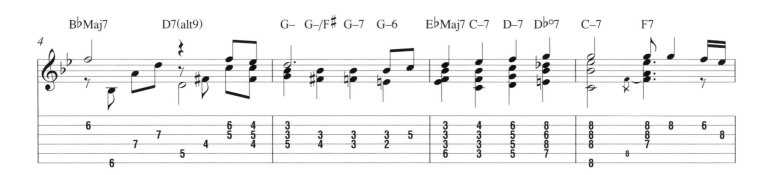

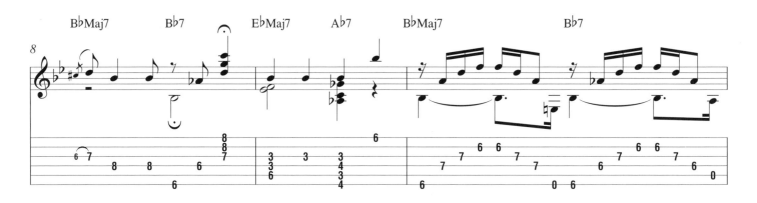

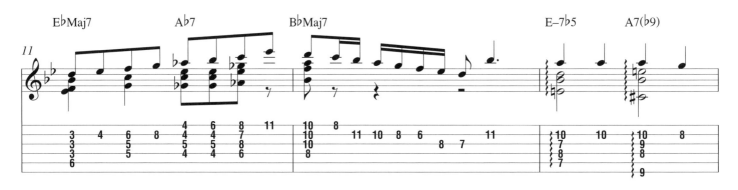

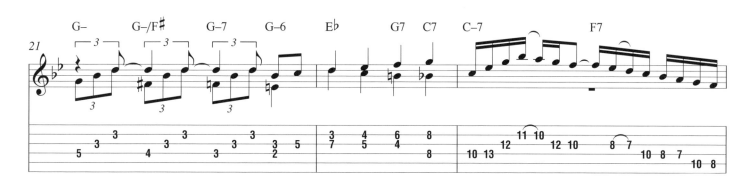

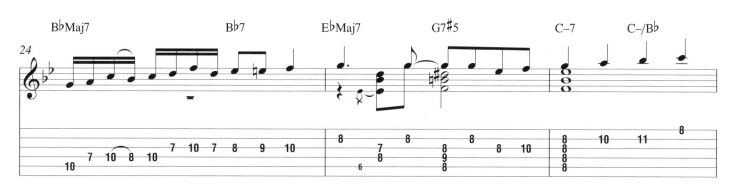

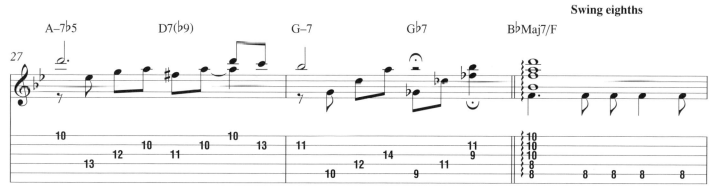

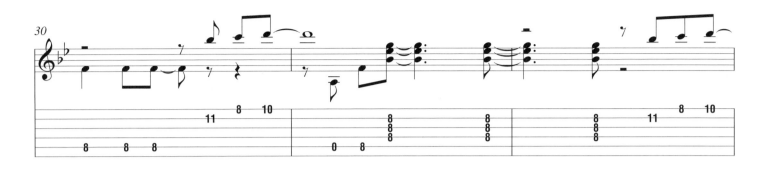

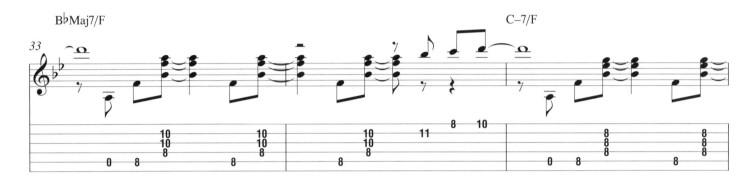

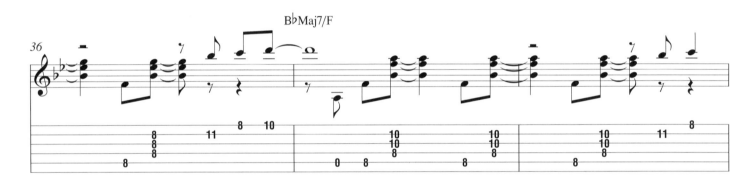

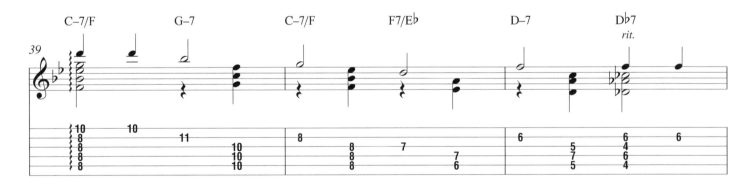

Out of Nowhere

"Out of Nowhere" is an example of a good "blowing tune." It is an ABAC tune with simple but effective harmony that doesn't particularly lend itself to fancy reharmonizations or re-imaginings, but is a lot of fun to improvise on. When I do solo gigs, I enjoy playing tunes like "Out of Nowhere," because they provide a nice jazzy contrast to the introspective ballad reharmonizations that otherwise tend to dominate a solo repertoire.

If one were playing a tune like "Out of Nowhere" in a group context, the obvious thing would be to play single-note lines over the accompaniment, but in a solo guitar format, it is necessary to do much more to maintain musical interest. The challenge of a blowing tune for solo guitar performance lies in finding a way to improvise on the tune and accompany oneself at the same time (or at least, maintain the illusion of the two simultaneous roles).

MIXING MELODIC LINES WITH CHORDS

There are a couple of tactics guitarists can use to simultaneously improvise and accompany themselves. One is to mix lines with chordal punctuations. A good way to understand how to do this is to listen to the way pianists comp for themselves during their solos. Of course, they sometimes reverse the roles their hands play, but generally they play melodic ideas in their right hand and use their left hand to drop in chords and other supportive musical material underneath the melody. As guitarists, we have to accomplish this in an efficient way, since we don't have the luxury of two independent hands. The concept is directly applicable, however, and it simply means we have to play shorter melodic phrases, pause to add some appropriate chordal comments, and then resume our melodies again.

It is important to know where we are in the tune at all times, so that we can break up our melodic phrases with the correct chords. By now, it is second nature for me, but I remember when playing like this was difficult simply because I did not always have a clear picture of the tune in my mind. It is very important to know the progressions thoroughly. Once we know the tune well, as we improvise we look for a spot to end a musical phrase, drop in a chord or two, and then we take a breath and resume the improvised line with a new phrase. Playing this way helps us focus on phrasing, which is extremely important, and the little chord punctuations in the pauses between our lines are a handy and musical way to separate and define our phrases, and to tie our improvisations closely to the chord progression of the tune.

HARMONIZING MELODIES WITH CHORDS

Another important technique for the solo guitarist is to improvise with harmonized lines—in other words, chords. We need thorough knowledge of voicings to accomplish this. The various chord tones, as well as the color notes in between the chord tones that are consonant with the chord, can be used as the highest note in a voicing with the rest of the chord underneath. We can take a melodic phrase and put a chord voicing under the important melody notes.

NOTES ON THE ARRANGEMENT

The arrangement begins with an introduction that is derived from the last melodic phrase of the tune, and then states the first chorus in a rubato manner. You will notice that much of the melody is played in single-note lines, with chord punctuations at the end of the phrases. Initially, the melody is played in a higher octave, and then moves down an octave. It's always easier to place the melody on the top strings of the guitar when we harmonize a tune because the notes in the chords can be added on the lower strings under the melody. When we mix melodic lines with chord punctuations, it becomes possible to play the melody in a lower octave and still use enough chords to give the impression of a harmonized melody.

The arrangement features improvisation in the second chorus, which starts on measure 25. Let's think about the harmony of the tune and look at how to approach improvising on "Out of Nowhere" as a solo guitarist. Here are the chords in the A sections of the tune:

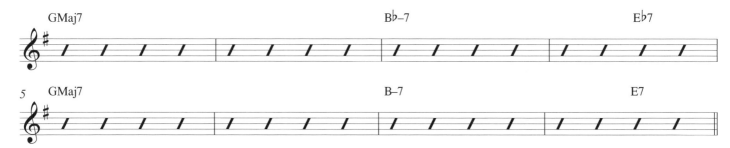

The first two measures of each 4-bar phrase in the A sections are harmonized with a GMaj7 chord (measures 25–26, 29–30, 41–42, 45–46). Since repetition is built into the harmony of the tune, repetition proved to be a valuable tool during the improvisation. I harmonized a little descending melodic phrase, alternating between GMaj7 (which is a stable sound) and either A–7 or D7 (unstable, thus creating tension that wants to resolve back to the GMaj7). This device repeats each time in the first two bars of the A sections.

The second two bars in each phrase in the A sections are harmonized with II V patterns: first, B♭–7 and E♭7, and then B–7 and E7. A melodic and rhythmic motif is repeated and sequenced in each of these 2-measure phrases (measures 27–28; 31–32; 43–44, 47–48). There is a melodic line in the first measure of each of these spots, and chords are dropped into the second measure.

Throughout the rest of the improvised second chorus, there is much use of melodic phrases, broken by chord punctuations.

The third chorus is a melody statement, this time in tempo and this time with the melody first in the lower octave, and then higher—just the reverse of the first chorus.

This arrangement of "Out of Nowhere" is an attempt to demonstrate how to approach a simple blowing tune in solo guitar performance. For practical reasons, the arrangement is limited to a version of the tune three choruses long. On a gig, one would most likely have played more choruses, and experimented more with the harmonies or even the form.

Track 8

Out of Nowhere

Arranged by
John Stein

Words by Edward Heyman
Music by Johnny Green

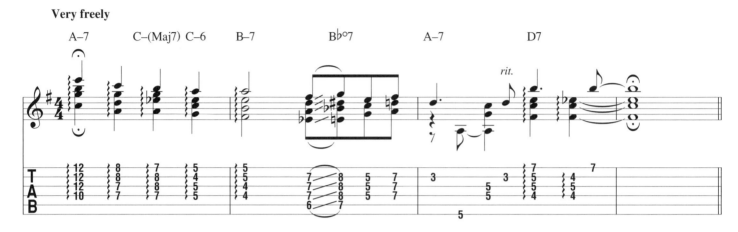

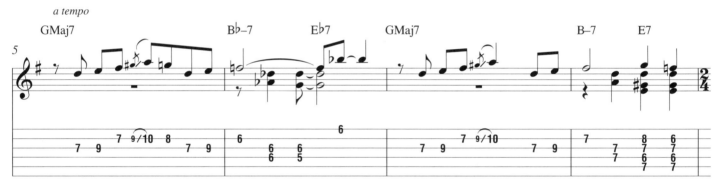

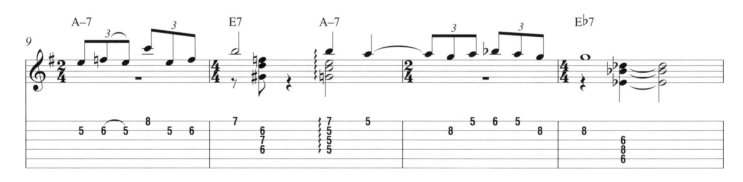

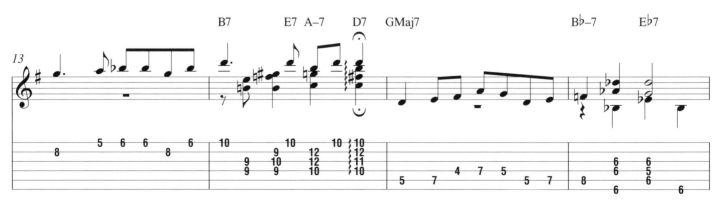

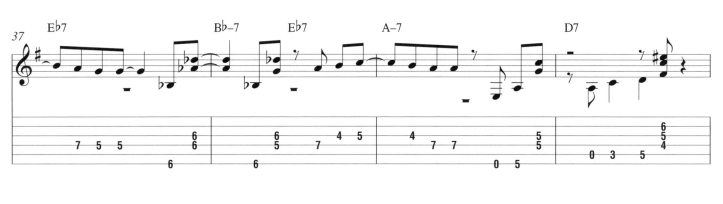

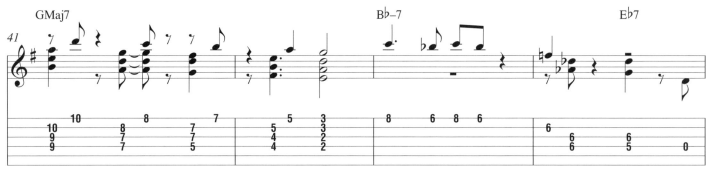

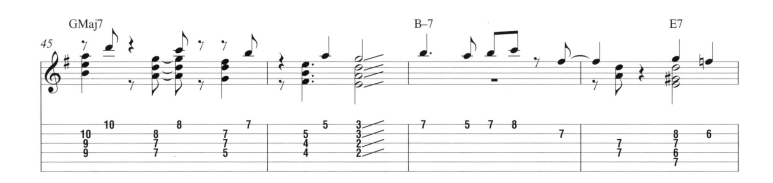

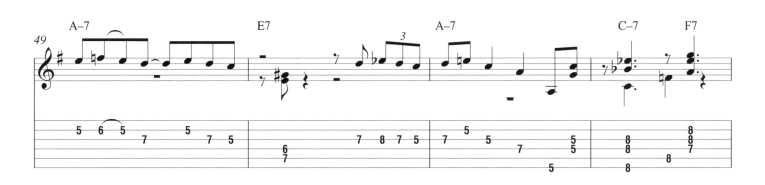

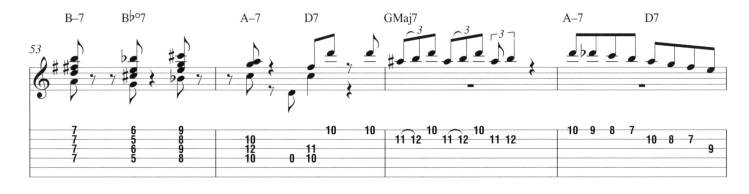

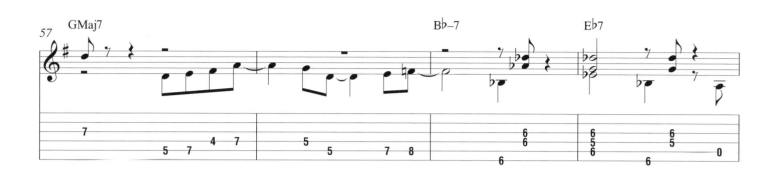

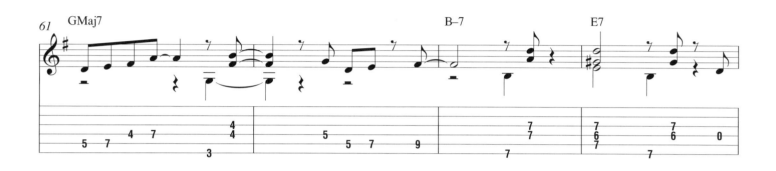

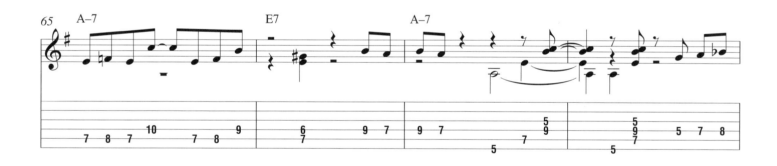

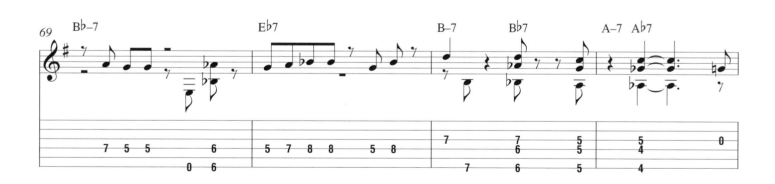

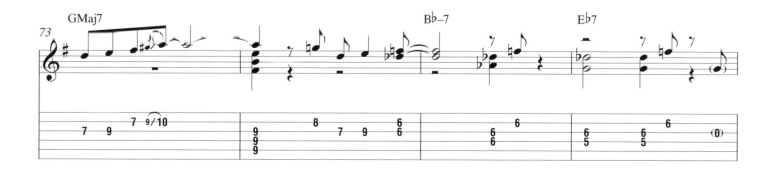

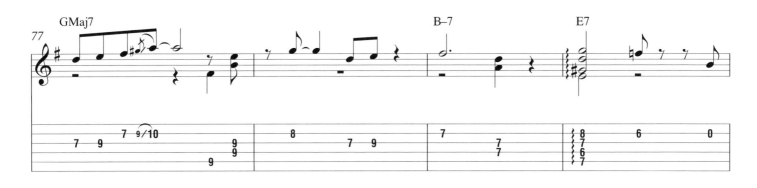

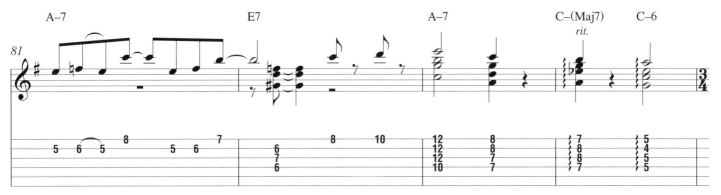

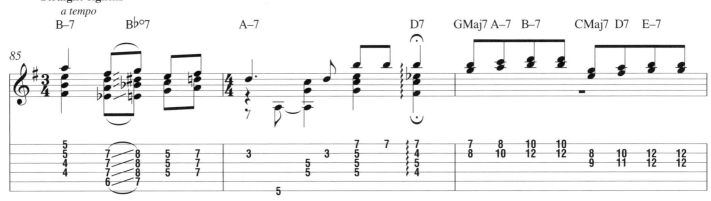

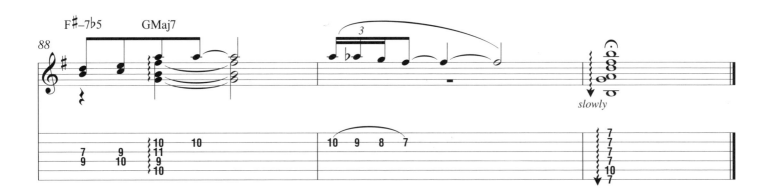

CHAPTER 9

Stella by Starlight

"Stella by Starlight" is one of the most popular and enduring of all the standard tunes. It was composed by Victor Young and appeared first as an instrumental theme song in *The Uninvited*, a 1944 film. Two years later, Ned Washington added lyrics, and both the Harry James Orchestra and Frank Sinatra had pop hits with their versions of the tune in 1947. Charlie Parker recorded the first jazz version of "Stella by Starlight" in 1952. Since Parker, it has been recorded thousands of times by jazz musicians.

"Stella By Starlight's" song form is quite unique: ABC. The A section of the tune contains a 16-bar phrase, while the B- and the C-sections are each 8 measures long. Each of the 8-bar sections has singular aspects. The B section features slower harmonic rhythm (two measures per chord), and the C section features descending minor II V's. The harmony in the A section is purposefully vague, as it begins on a ♯IV–7♭5 chord and manages to avoid the tonic chord until measure 9 of the tune, which is bar 13 in this arrangement. Even then, the B♭ chord passes by so quickly that the tonality is barely established.

There is something magical about Victor Young's use of the ♯IV–7♭5 chord. It is the first chord we hear, and it appears twice more in the meandering A section phrase. In measure 10 (measure 14 of the arrangement), it is part of a cadence to the D–7 chord, and it appears in measure 14 (measure 18 of the arrangement) in the transition to the B section of the tune. Victor Young even chooses to use the chord an additional time. He begins the descending patterns in the C section with it.

The ♯IV–7♭5 does not come from the tonality of a song in a major key, but it is often used along with key-related chords in several cliché patterns. We recognize the chord when we hear it, but its slightly vague relationship to the tonal center makes it perfect for the abstraction in the A section of "Stella by Starlight." I think the repetition of this chord is part of the glue that allows such an unorthodox song form to hang together and make musical sense.

This arrangement is two choruses long. In the first chorus, the melody occurs in the lower octave, mostly in single notes with chord punctuations.

When the melody is primarily on the G, D, or A strings, it is difficult to add harmony notes under the melody. The solution is to play a melodic phrase, and then leave some space to drop in a couple of chords. The second chorus occurs an octave higher, with the melody notes on the B and E strings. Although I continue to employ the technique of playing single-note melodic phrases with chordal punctuations, it is much easier to place voicings under a melody on the higher strings. It is important to remember where you are in the tune, in order to drop the right chords into the appropriate spots. Also notice how small the voicings often are. Two or three notes are enough to imply the harmony.

I think one of the reasons "Stella by Starlight" has a strong appeal for jazz musicians is that its unusual form and meandering progression is quite a challenge. There are a lot of chords to remember, and no repetition in the form to make it easier. Sometimes, when I'm in the mood to challenge myself, I take a tune like this, which I've learned in the original tonality, and I try to play it in another key. It requires a lot of concentration!

Track 9

Stella by Starlight

Arranged by
John Stein

Words by Ned Washington
Music by Victor Young

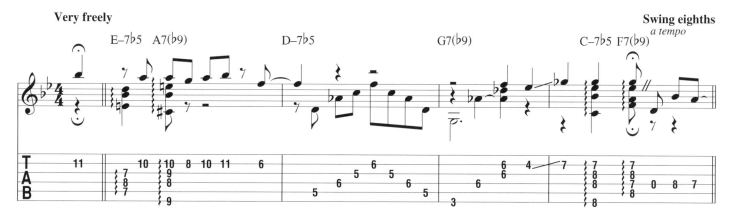

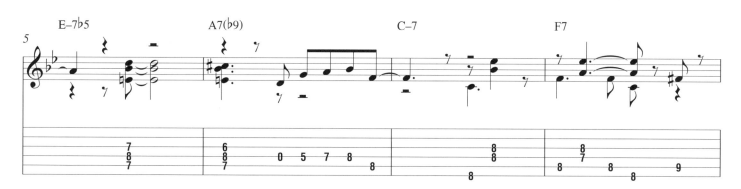

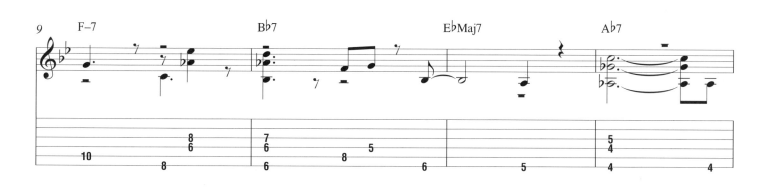

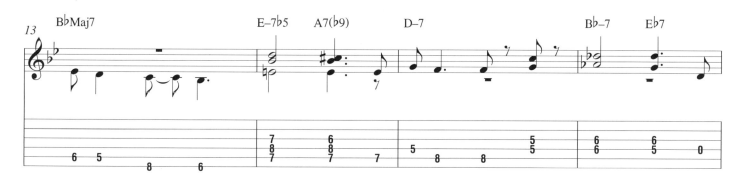

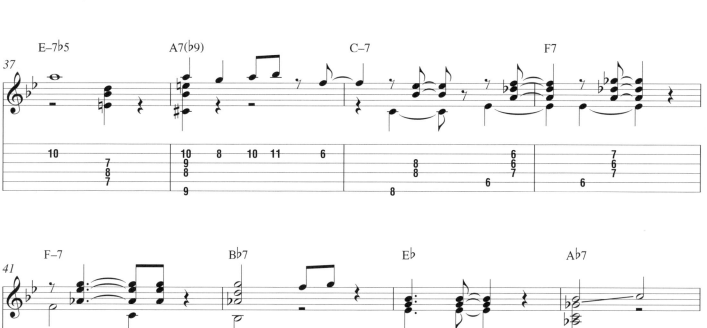
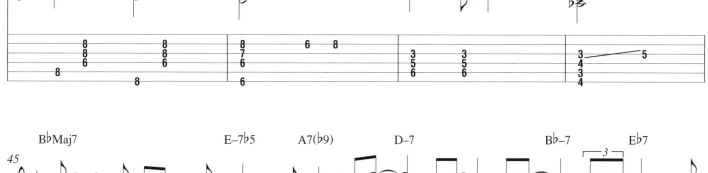
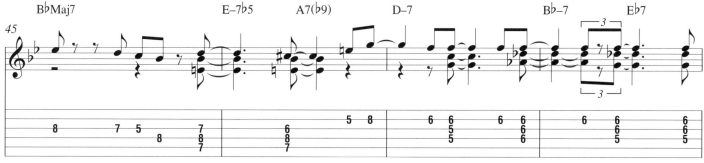
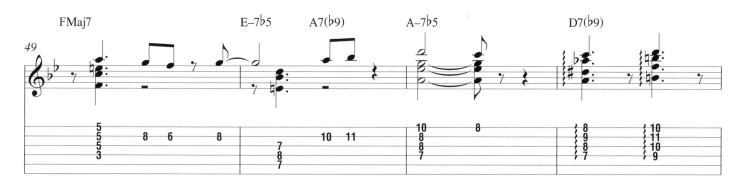
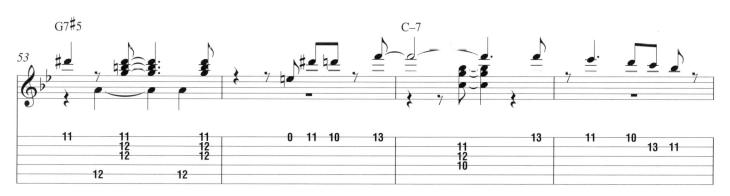

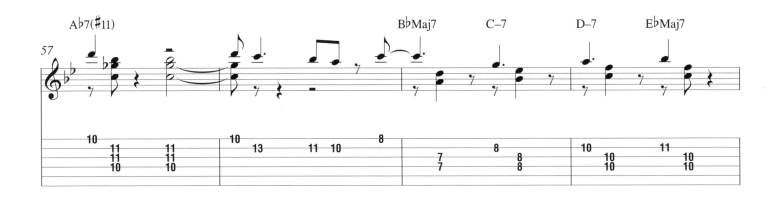

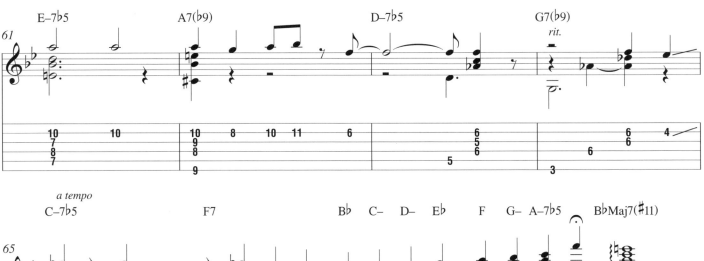

CHAPTER 10

You Don't Know
What Love Is

This tune utilizes an AABA song form. The first decision an arranger must make is how to provide contrast during the many repetitions of the A sections. This arrangement features reharmonization of the basic chord changes and organizes the first two A sections around descending and ascending bass lines.

"You Don't Know What Love Is" is written in the key of F minor, but the arrangement takes liberty with the original chords and begins each of the first two A sections in the relative major tonality: A♭ major. During the first A section, the bass line descends from the E natural in measure 2 chromatically to the A♭ in measure 6, each bass note harmonized by a chord that creates tension, then resolves downward to a more stable chord until we reach the end of the phrase. The second A section features a harmonized ascending bass line, beginning on the A♭ chord in measure 9 and rising chromatically to the D♭7 chord in measure 12.

The final A section begins and ends in the composer's tonality of F minor and features the original chords, embellished only by the bittersweet sound of available tensions (the extensions of the chords).

The arrangement is heightened by the contrast between the first half of the tune performed freely out of tempo, and the second half of the tune played with a swinging double-time feel.

My favorite moment in this composition occurs in the B section. The original chords in the A sections are in the tonality of F minor. As often happens in minor key music, the B section modulates to the relative major key (A♭ major) for contrast. The truly unique event in this tune occurs in measures 25 through 28, where the composer adds an additional modulation, this time to the unrelated tonality of C major. There is also an unrepeated high point in the melody in measure 25, the E natural note. It is simultaneously the highest note in the melody, as well as the note with the most contrast between the tonalities of F minor/A♭ major and C major. Very clever, and of course, it sounds wonderful! In classical western melody-writing tradition, an unrepeated high note is desirable, as it serves as a climax point.

Track 10

You Don't Know What Love Is

Arranged by
John Stein

Words and Music by Don Raye
and Gene DePaul

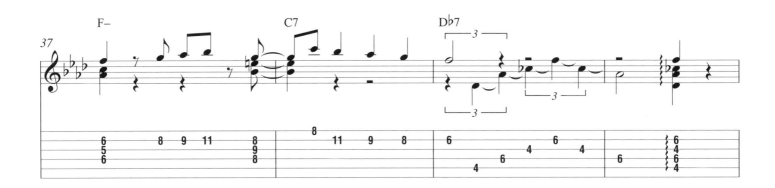

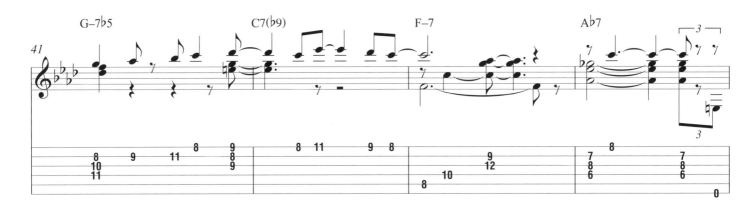

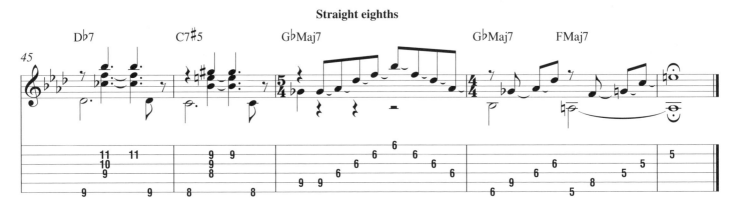

ABOUT THE AUTHOR

Photo by Kofi

Internationally renowned jazz guitarist John Stein was born and raised in Kansas City, Missouri, where he took up his instrument at an early age. His talent for and love of music ultimately earned him a faculty position at Berklee College of Music in Boston, where he is an associate professor in the Harmony Department. John has performed as a leader or a sideman with some of America's finest jazz acts. His compositions and performances cover the spectrum of jazz, from blues to bebop to bossas to swing. John has toured in the United States as well as in Brazil, Germany, France, and Switzerland. John has published educational columns in *Just Jazz Guitar* magazine for many years. Along with this book of solo guitar arrangements, he has compiled his educational materials into two additional books: *Composing Blues for Jazz Performance* and *Composing Tunes for Jazz Performance*.

RECORDINGS

Bing Bang Boom! with John Lockwood, Jake Sherman, Zé Eduardo Nazario. Whaling City Sound, WCS 062 (2013).

Concerto Internacional de Jazz, with Bocato, Teco Cardoso, Alexandre Zamith, Frank Herzberg, Zé Eduardo Nazario. Whaling City Sound, WCS 031 (2006).

Conversation Pieces, with David "Fathead" Newman, Keala Kaumeheiwa, Greg Conroy. Jardis Records, JRCD 20140 (2001).

Encounterpoint, with John Lockwood, Koichi Sato, Zé Eduardo Nazario. Whaling City Sound, WCS 042 (2008).

Green Street, with David "Fathead" Newman, Ken Clark, David Hurst. Whaling City Sound, WCS 039 (1999, reissued 2007).

Hi Fly, with John Lockwood, Jake Sherman, Zé Eduardo Nazario. Whaling City Sound, WCS 054 (2011).

Hustle Up! with Les Harris, Sr., David Hurst, David Limina, Bruce Torff, Marshall Wood. TightlyKnit Records, KFW 172 (1995).

Interplay, with John Lockwood, Yoron Israel. Azica Records, AJD 72226 (2004).

Portraits and Landscapes, with Larry Goldings, Bill Thompson, Keala Kaumeheiwa, Greg Conroy. Jardis Records, JRCD 20029 (2000).

Raising the Roof, with John Lockwood, Koichi Sato, Zé Eduardo Nazario. Whaling City Sound, WCS 050 (2010).

Turn Up the Quiet, with Ron Gill, Gilad Barkan. Whaling City Sound, WCS 051 (2010).

QUOTES

"John Stein is the poet of the classical jazz guitar."
—Dick Crockett, "The Voice," 88.7 FM

"John Stein is one of the great guitarists, in the tradition of Joe Pass and Tal Farlow."
—Ron Della Chiesa, WPLM, 99.1 FM

"What a gift this man has. He's in an elite class: a mere handful of jazz guitarists who consistently put taste above chops and flash. John Stein has the ability to say so much more with less effort than most of his contemporaries can muster."
—Wayne Everett Goins, KC JAM

"John Stein is one of the finest jazz guitarists you'll ever hear, with beautiful touch, tone, swing, detail, and emotion. There's a wealth of detail—the dips and turns of phrases, accents falling like words that he gets at even the fastest tempos."
—Jon Garelick, *The Boston Phoenix*

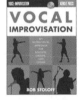